I0644337

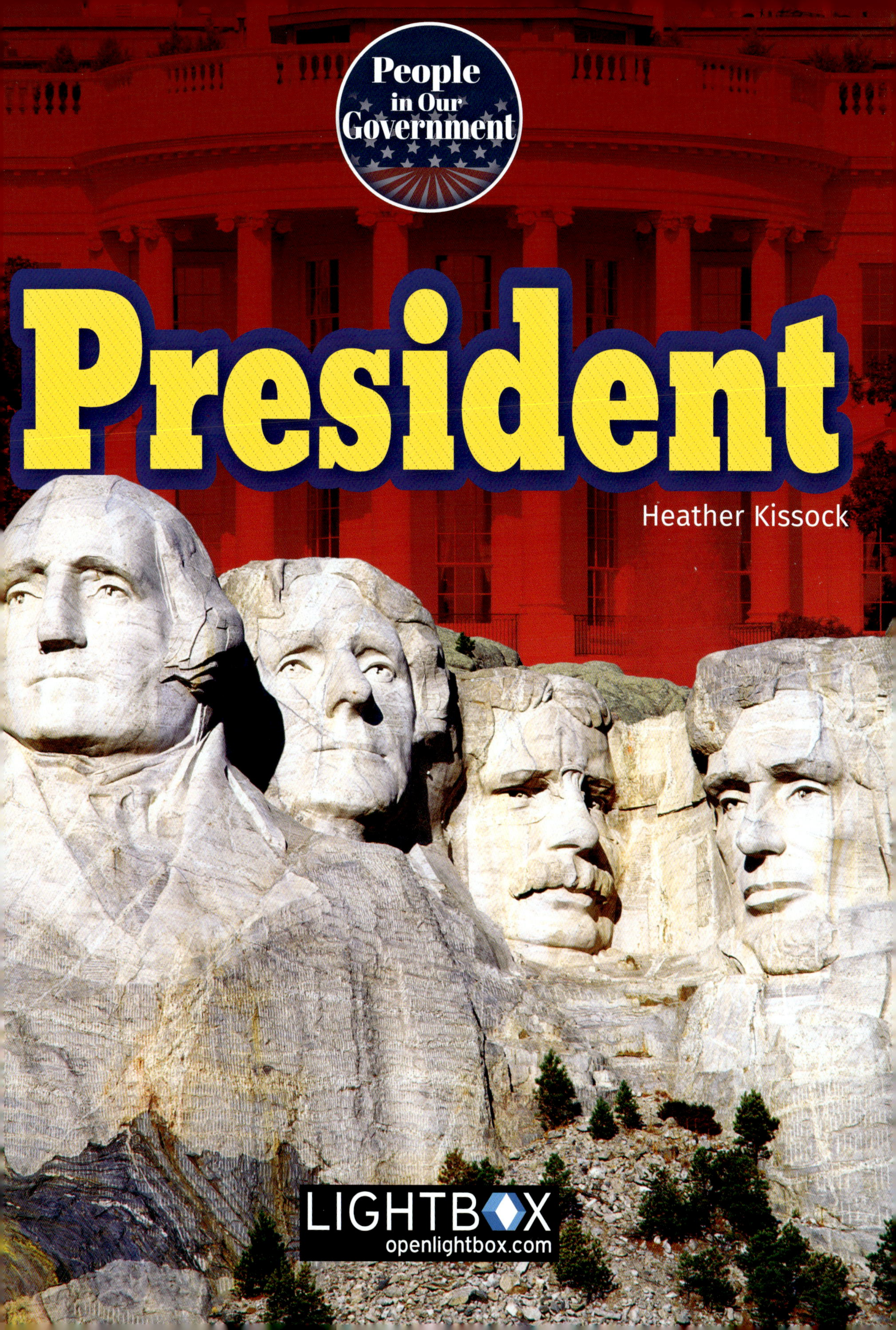

People in Our Government

President

Heather Kissock

LIGHTBOX
openlightbox.com

LIGHTBOX

Go to **www.openlightbox.com** and enter this book's unique code.

ACCESS CODE

LBXG5466

Lightbox is an all-inclusive digital solution for the teaching and learning of curriculum topics in an original, groundbreaking way. Lightbox is based on National Curriculum Standards.

STANDARD FEATURES OF LIGHTBOX

AUDIO High-quality narration using text-to-speech system

ACTIVITIES Printable PDFs that can be emailed and graded

SLIDESHOWS Pictorial overviews of key concepts

VIDEOS Embedded high-definition video clips

WEBLINKS Curated links to external, child-safe resources

TRANSPARENCIES Step-by-step layering of maps, diagrams, charts, and timelines

INTERACTIVE MAPS Interactive maps and aerial satellite imagery

QUIZZES Ten multiple choice questions that are automatically graded and emailed for teacher assessment

KEY WORDS Matching key concepts to their definitions

Copyright © 2021 Smartbook Media Inc. All rights reserved.

President

Contents

Who Is the President?

The president of the United States is the head of state. This means that he or she is the top leader in the country's government. The president is also in charge of the U.S. armed forces. These groups help keep the country safe.

The United States has had 45 presidents. The first president was George Washington. He led the country from 1789 to 1797. Washington played a key role in building the new country and its government. This is why he is often called the "Father of His Country."

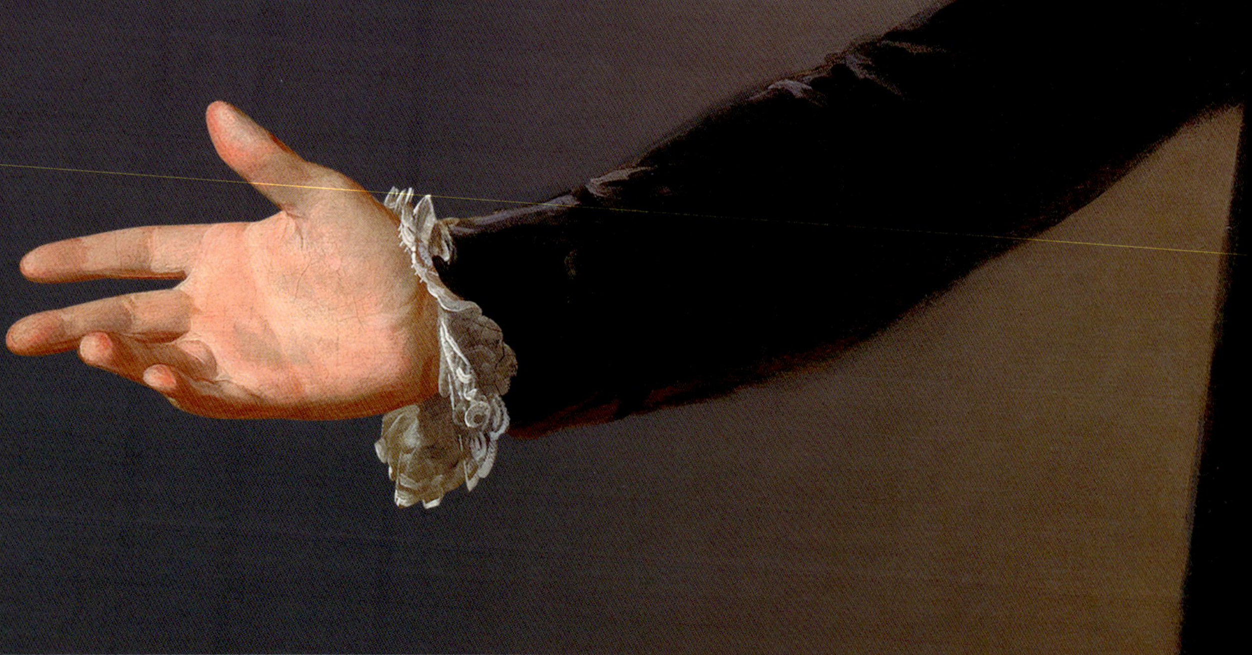

Although George Washington was asked to serve a third term as president, he declined. He did not want the president to rule for a lifetime, like a king would.

The Government

The U.S. government is described in the Constitution. This document was written to establish the new country and its laws. The Constitution explains the three branches of government. Each branch has its own role. Together, they take care of the country and its people.

The legislative branch makes the country's laws. The executive branch carries out the laws. The judicial branch settles any problems with the country's laws.

The three branches of the U.S. government are all based in Washington, D.C. This is the country's capital.

Structure of the U.S. Government

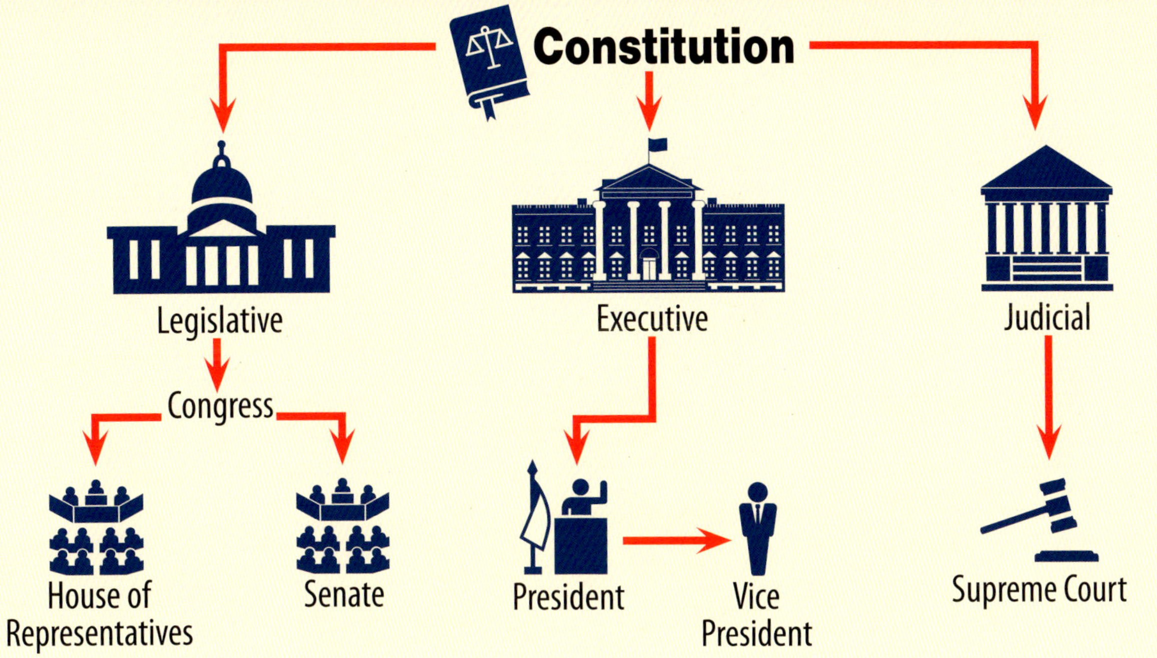

The Role

The president is in charge of the executive branch. Everyone who works in this branch reports to him or her. The president must keep track of what these people are doing. He or she needs to know they are working to help the country.

Another job the president has is to choose people for important jobs. These include **ambassadors** and judges. The president also signs important papers. In 1867, President Andrew Johnson signed the Alaska Treaty. This made Alaska part of the United States.

Presidents meet with ambassadors to learn more about relations with other countries.

Many people thought purchasing Alaska was a poor idea, but they were proven wrong. Today, Alaska is a popular tourist destination.

The United States paid **$7.2 million** for Alaska.

Andrew Johnson was the country's **17th president**.

Theodore Roosevelt is known for helping protect the environment and involving the United States more in world politics.

What It Takes

A person must meet certain rules to become president. He or she must have been born in the United States. Someone who wants to become president must have lived in the country for at least 14 years. No one under the age of 35 can be president.

Theodore Roosevelt was the youngest person to become president. He was 42 years old at the time. Roosevelt took on the role in 1901 when President William McKinley died.

The president must be a U.S. citizen. Anyone born in the United States is a citizen of that country.

Getting the Job

A president is **elected** every four years. However, becoming president does not happen quickly. There are several steps involved.

1

Candidates from each **political party** travel the country to gain support. Party members in each state choose the candidate they want to be president.

2

Large meetings are held. Each political party chooses one person to run for president.

3 These **nominees** travel across the country. They make speeches and try to get support.

4 People across the country vote for the person they think should be president. Their votes are called the popular vote.

5 Each state has people called electors. The votes of the electors decide which candidate becomes president. The person with the highest popular vote in each state gets that state's electoral votes. The person with the most electoral votes across the country becomes president.

The White House

The White House is the official home of the president. This building is found in Washington, D.C. The White House is not just a home. Inside are the offices for the president and his or her staff. There are also rooms for special events.

The State Floor
This is the first floor of the White House. It features the Blue Room. The president uses this room to greet guests. The State Dining Room is also on this floor.

The State Dining Room can seat up to **140 people.**

The White House has **132** rooms, **35** bathrooms, **412** doors, and **28** fireplaces.

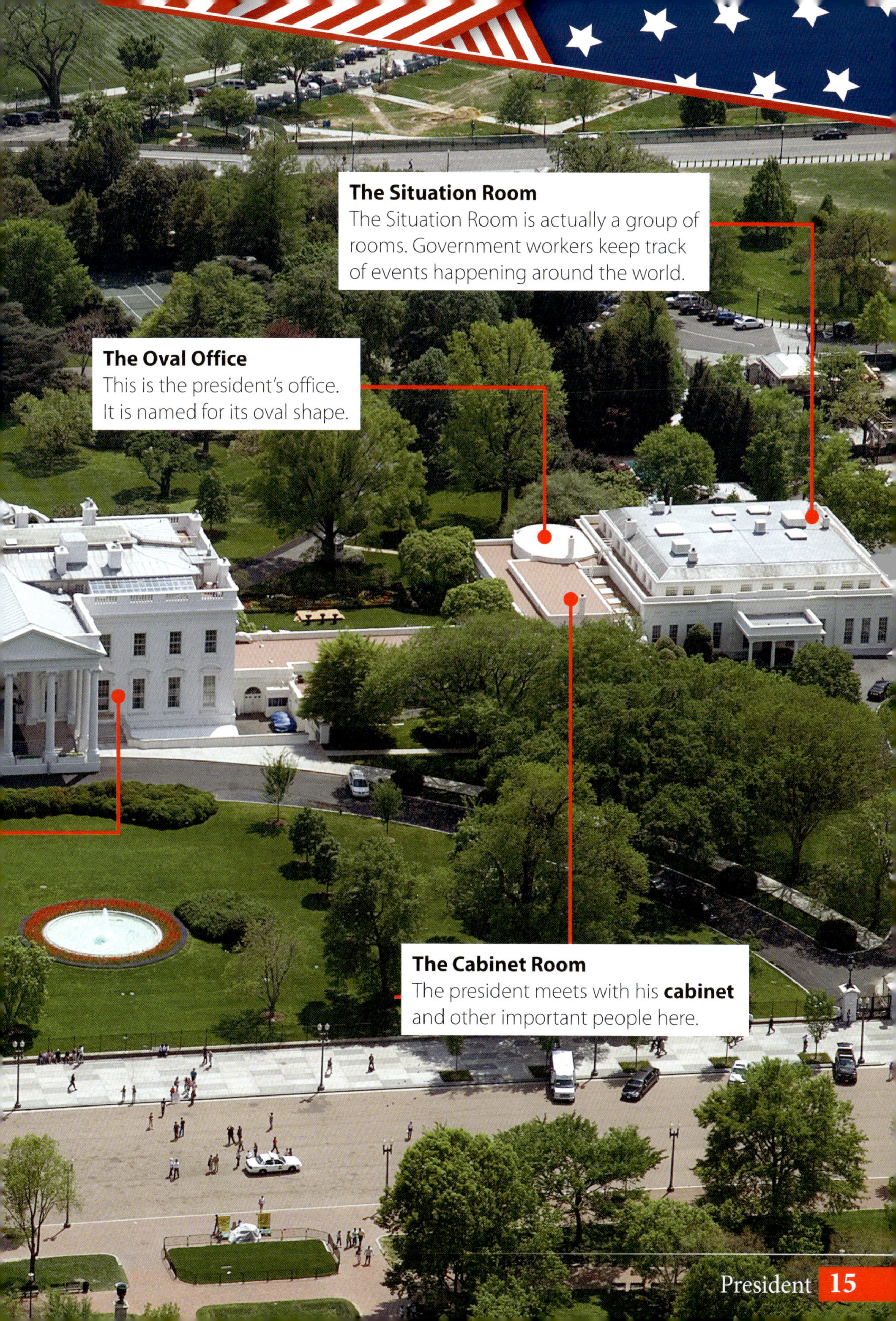
The Situation Room
The Situation Room is actually a group of rooms. Government workers keep track of events happening around the world.
The Oval Office
This is the president's office. It is named for its oval shape.
The Cabinet Room
The president meets with his **cabinet** and other important people here.

Leading in Public

Americans look to the president to lead them. The president must keep in touch with them. This is done in a variety of ways.

The president visits states that have been impacted by a natural disaster, such as a hurricane or tornado.

Visits to States

The president travels around the country. He or she speaks with Americans to learn about their problems. The president then returns to Washington to address their concerns.

State of the Union Address

The president gives the State of the Union Address from the House Chamber in the U.S. Capitol Building.

Every year, the president gives a speech about the country. He or she talks about what has been achieved in the last year and what issues need to be addressed in the coming year. This speech is watched on television by tens of millions of people.

Presidents talk with world leaders in one-on-one meetings, as well as at large gatherings of leaders.

Meets with World Leaders

Helping to solve big problems is part of a president's job. He or she meets with world leaders. They try to resolve issues that affect both the world and the United States.

Celebrates American Victories

The president supports American sports teams. He or she often invites winning teams to the White House. This includes winners of events such as the Super Bowl or the World Series.

The winning team often gives the president a personalized jersey when it visits the White House.

A Day in the Life

The president is a busy person. A president's work never really stops. Each day is filled with questions that need answers.

The president participates in meetings and signs important paperwork at his desk in the Oval Office.

8:00 am

The president and his secretary meet to go over the plans for the day.

9:00 am

The president meets with the head of the National Security Agency. He is given an update on its work.

11:00 am

The governor of Louisiana meets with the president. They discuss the steps being taken to recover from a recent hurricane.

2:00 pm

The president holds a **press conference** to talk about a new **trade** agreement.

4:00 pm

The afternoon includes meetings with the president's staff. There are problems to discuss, such as how to plan a new law.

8:00 pm

The president calls the leader of another country. They discuss how each country can help the other.

Notable Presidents

Presidents are remembered for what they did while in office. Many have taken important actions to help the country grow. Some have also helped the world as a whole.

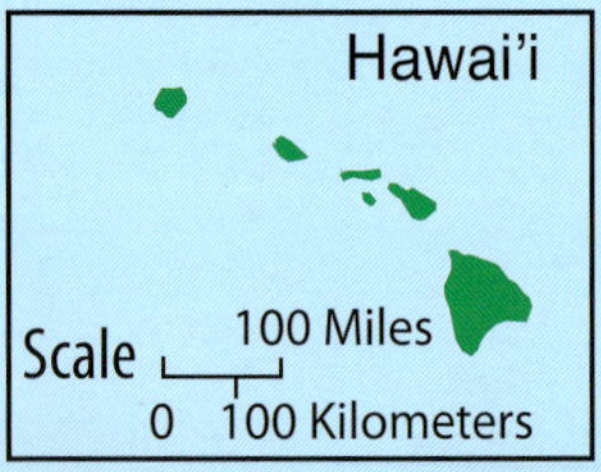

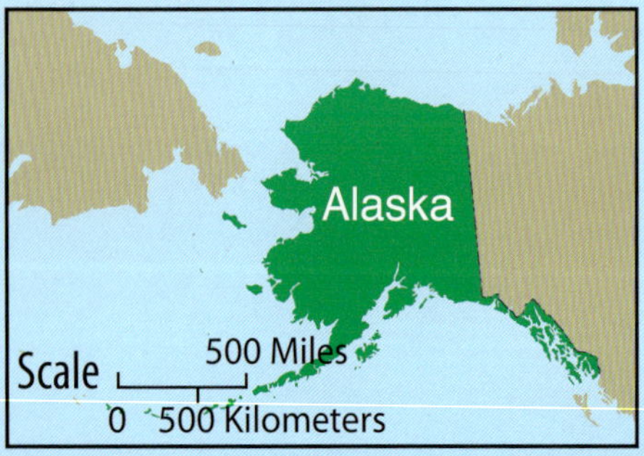

Dwight D. Eisenhower

Years in Office:

1953–1961

Eisenhower is best known for founding **NASA**. He also brought an end to the Korean War. Eisenhower believed in world peace.

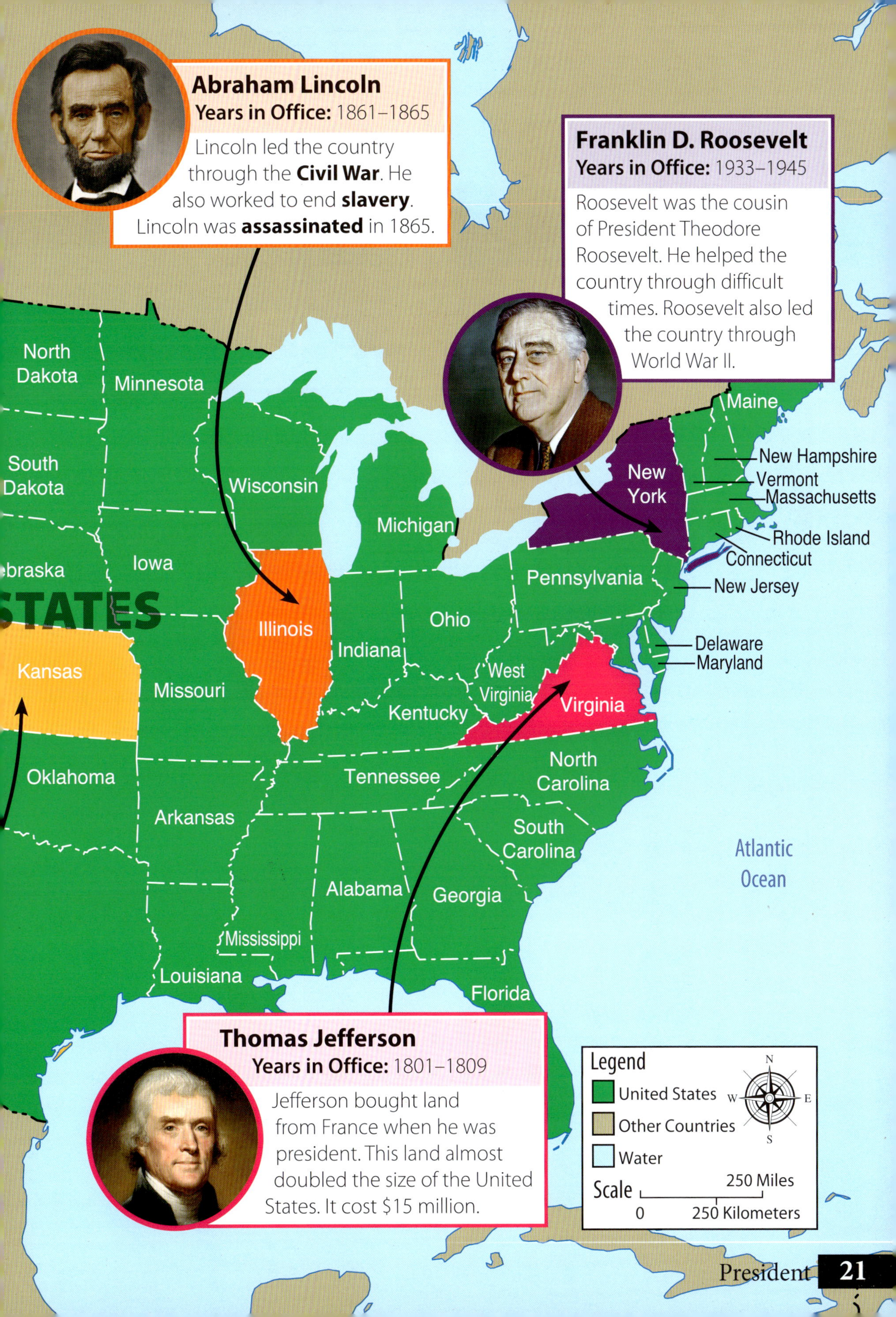

Abraham Lincoln

Years in Office: 1861–1865

Lincoln led the country through the **Civil War**. He also worked to end **slavery**. Lincoln was **assassinated** in 1865.

Franklin D. Roosevelt

Years in Office: 1933–1945

Roosevelt was the cousin of President Theodore Roosevelt. He helped the country through difficult times. Roosevelt also led the country through World War II.

Thomas Jefferson

Years in Office: 1801–1809

Jefferson bought land from France when he was president. This land almost doubled the size of the United States. It cost $15 million.

Quiz

1 Who was the first president of the United States?

2 Who is in charge of the executive branch of the U.S. government?

3 How old must someone be to become president?

4 How often is a president elected?

5 What is the State of the Union Address?

6 Which president founded NASA?

ANSWERS

1 George Washington **2** The president **3** At least 35 years old **4** Every four years **5** A speech the president gives about issues facing the country and how to address them **6** Dwight D. Eisenhower

Key Words

ambassadors: people who represent their country in another country

assassinated: murdered for political reasons

cabinet: a group of people that gives advice to a leader

candidates: people who seek or are put forward for a job

Civil War: the war between the northern and southern states between 1861 and 1865

elected: voted into a job

NASA: the National Aeronautics and Space Administration, an organization that studies and explores space

nominees: people who are formally entered as a candidate for political office

political party: a group of people who share the same views about the way power should be used in a country

press conference: an event organized to provide information and answer questions from the media

slavery: the practice of owning a person

trade: the business of buying and selling goods

Index

LIGHTBOX

SUPPLEMENTARY RESOURCES

Click on the plus icon found in the bottom left corner of each spread to open additional teacher resources.

- Download and print the book's quizzes and activities
- Access curriculum correlations
- Explore additional web applications that enhance the Lightbox experience

LIGHTBOX DIGITAL TITLES

Packed full of integrated media

VIDEOS

INTERACTIVE MAPS

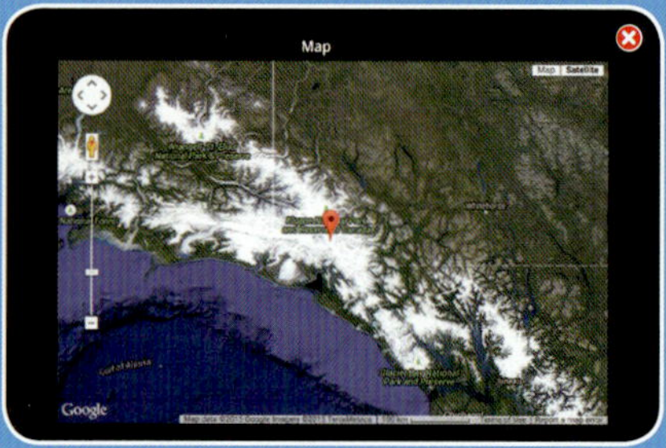

WEBLINKS

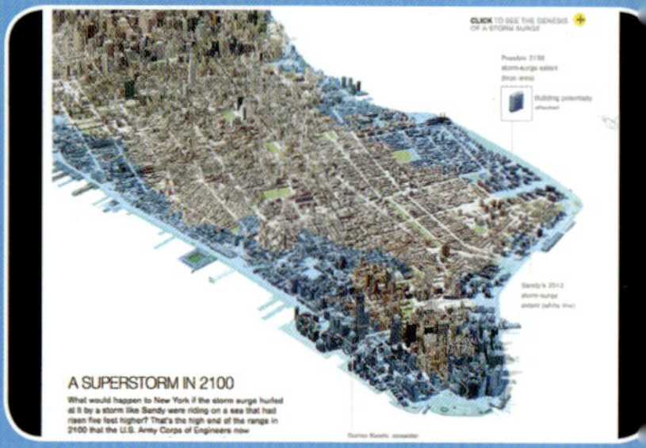

SLIDESHOWS

QUIZZES

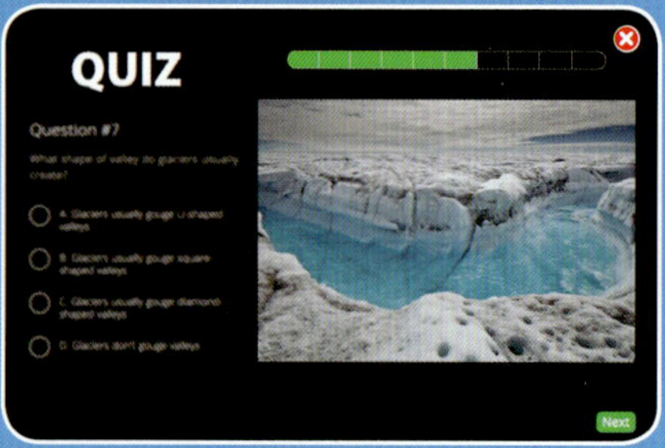

OPTIMIZED FOR

- ✔ TABLETS
- ✔ WHITEBOARDS
- ✔ COMPUTERS
- ✔ AND MUCH MORE!

Published by Smartbook Media Inc.
14 Penn Plaza 9th Floor
New York, NY 10122
Website: www.openlightbox.com

Copyright © 2021 Smartbook Media Inc.
All rights reserved. No part of this publication may be reproduced, stored in a retrieval system, or transmitted in any form or by any means, electronic, mechanical, photocopying, recording, or otherwise, without the prior written permission of the publisher.

Library of Congress Control Number: 2020938416

ISBN 978-1-5105-5456-6 (hardcover)
ISBN 978-1-5105-5457-3 (multi-user eBook)

Printed in Guangzhou, China
1 2 3 4 5 6 7 8 9 0 24 23 22 21 20

062020
111019

Project Coordinator Heather Kissock
Designer Ana María Vidal

Photo Credits
Every reasonable effort has been made to trace ownership and to obtain permission to reprint copyright material. The publisher would be pleased to have any errors or omissions brought to its attention so that they may be corrected in subsequent printings. The publisher acknowledges Getty Images, Shutterstock, and iStock as its primary image suppliers for this title.